MW00748096

Bible-based activities to strengthen Christian values

All puzzles and Bible activities are based on the NIV.

Scripture taken from the Holy Bible, New International Version, Copyright ©1973, 1978, 1984, International Bible Society. Used by permission of Zondervan Bible Publishers.

ISBN: 0-7814-5101-9

Edited by Debbie Bible
Book Design by Jack Rogers
Cover Illustration by Corbin Hillam
Interior Illustrations by Dana Regan & Corbin Hillam

TABLE OF CONTENTS

INTRODUCTION FOR ADULT FRIENDS OF CHILDREN
(Parents, Teachers, and Other Friends of Children)

Values. What are they? How do we acquire them? Can we change them? "Values" is a popular term, usually meaning *the standard that governs how one acts and conducts one's life.* Our personal standards, or values, are learned and adapted, possibly changed and relearned, over a lifetime of experiences and influences. Children begin acquiring personal values at birth. As parents, teachers, and other adults who love children, we are concerned that they are learning worthwhile values, rather than being randomly influenced by everything around them. By God's design, we cannot control the process of acquiring values, but we can influence the process in a variety of ways. Our consistent modeling of biblical values is a vital influence, but children must also be encouraged to talk about specific values and be aware of these values in action in themselves and others.

These biblical values are God's values. He has established His standards to help us know how to live our lives and how we are to treat other people. Our goal is to have these biblical values be a part of each child's experience.

A value becomes one's own when a person chooses to act on that value consistently. Saying that we hold to the value of honesty, yet bending the truth or telling a lie when pressured, is a contradiction.

Providing opportunities for children to investigate a specific value, identifying with people in the Bible who have that value, and trying to put it into practice in real life situations will help strengthen the value in the lives of the children and reinforce its importance. The purpose of the Value Builders Series is to provide such opportunities.

This book in the Value Builders Series focuses on **being kind** and **being purposeful**. Being kind is *doing something nice or helpful for another person.* King David was kind to Mephibosheth, Jonathan's son, and not only returned land to him but also invited him to come out of hiding and eat at the king's table every day. Paul is another biblical example of being kind. He was with a large group of people who safely survived a shipwreck. The islanders welcomed them warmly and kindly provided for them for three months.

Being purposeful is *knowing what you want to do and being determined to do it.* When Jesus was in Gethsemane, facing the agony of the cross, He was purposeful about His decision to follow His Father's will instead of wishing to escape from

great pain. Joshua is another example for us. He was purposeful in his decision to serve and obey God.

The Value Builders Series provides Bible story activities, craft activities, and life application activities that focus on specific biblical values. These books can be used by children working alone, or the pages can be reproduced and used in a classroom setting.

In a classroom setting, this book could be used to supplement curriculum that you are using, or it can be used as a curriculum itself in a 30-55 minute period. Each page is coded at the bottom to suggest where it might fit in a teaching session. The codes are as follows:

 = Definition page

 = Bible Story page

= Craft page

 = Life Application page

Some suggestions for using the materials in this book in a 30-55 minute period are:

5-10 minutes:	Introduce the value and discuss the definition. Use pages entitled, "What Is Being Kind?" or "What Is Being Purposeful?"
10-15 minutes:	Present one of the Bible stories, using appropriate pages. Encourage the children to describe what it might have been like to be in that situation and what other things could have happened.
10-20 minutes:	Choose life application activity pages or craft activities that are appropriate to the children in your class. Design some group applications for the pages you have chosen.
5-10 minutes:	To conclude, use the page entitled, "The Value of Being Kind" or "The Value of Being Purposeful" and encourage the children to make a commitment to focus on this value for the next few days or weeks. Pray for God's help to guide the children as they learn to live by His standards.

WHAT IS BEING KIND?

BEING KIND IS...**doing something nice or helpful for another person.**

I think being kind can also mean _____

_____

One kind thing I like to do for someone is _____

_____

One kind thing I like someone to do for me is _____

_____

Being kind is important to me.
When I spend time doing something nice or helpful for another person, then being kind becomes one of my values.

Name _____

Date _____

God's values are the STANDARD to help me know how to live my life and treat other people

David Is Kind to Mephibosheth

King Saul was dead and David was the new king. Saul's relatives were hiding, just in case King David would try to kill them to keep them from trying to become king.

2 Samuel 9:1-13

David asked, "Is there anyone still left of the house of Saul to whom I can show kindness for Jonathan's sake?"

Now there was a servant of Saul's household named Ziba. They called him to appear before David, and the king said to him, "Are you Ziba?"

"Your servant," he replied.

The king asked, "Is there no one still left of the house of Saul to whom I can show God's kindness?"

Ziba answered the king, "There is still a son of Jonathan; he is crippled in both feet."

"Where is he?" the king asked.

Ziba answered, "He is at the house of Makir son of Ammiel in Lo Debar."

So King David had him brought from Lo Debar, from the house of Makir son of Ammiel.

When Mephibosheth son of Jonathan, the son of Saul, came to David, he bowed down to pay him honor.

David said, "Mephibosheth!"

"[I am] your servant," he replied.

(Read the rest of the story on page 7)

Mephibosheth has been hiding so he will not be killed by the new king. Ziba knows how to find him. Ziba is going to Lo Debar to bring Mephibosheth to King David. Can you find the way that Ziba will take? ✏️ **Trace Ziba's route from the palace to Lo Debar and then come back to the palace by a different route.**

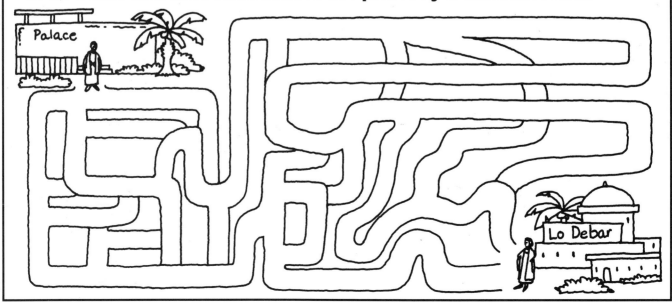

David Is Kind to Mephibosheth

(2 Samuel 9:1-13 continued from page 6)

"Don't be afraid," David said to him, "for I will surely show you kindness for the sake of your father Jonathan. I will restore to you all the land that belonged to your grandfather Saul, and you will always eat at my table."

"RESTORE" IS TO MAKE IT LIKE IT USED TO BE.

Mephibosheth bowed down and said, "What am [I], that you should notice a dead dog like me?"

"SUMMONED" IS ORDERING SOMEONE TO COME.

Then the king summoned Ziba, Saul's servant, and said to him, "I have given your master's grandson everything that belonged to Saul and his family. You and your sons and your servants are to farm the land for him and bring in the crops, so that your master's grandson may be provided for. And Mephibosheth, grandson of your master, will always eat at my table." (Now Ziba had fifteen sons and twenty servants.)

Then Ziba said to the king, "[I] will do whatever my lord the king commands [me] to do." So Mephibosheth ate at David's table like one of the king's sons.

Mephibosheth had a young son named Mica, and all the members of Ziba's household were servants of Mephibosheth. And Mephibosheth lived in Jerusalem, because he always ate at the king's table, and he was crippled in both feet.

✎ **Cross out the letters that spell the name of the picture. Write the rest of the letters on the line with the same number.**

1. dhaormg

2. tlraende

3. linvoitcedk

4. rienatg

King David was kind when he . . . didn't _____ the former king's family,
1

gave back the _____ to Mephibosheth, and
2

_____ Mephibosheth to _____ at the palace.
3   4

THE BIBLE TELLS ABOUT BEING KIND

David Is Kind to Mephibosheth

Read about David and Mephibosheth in your Bible in 2 Samuel 9:1-13 or on pages 6 and 7. ✎ **Look in the Bible story to find out about each person. Draw the correct picture or write the name in the box beside each description.**

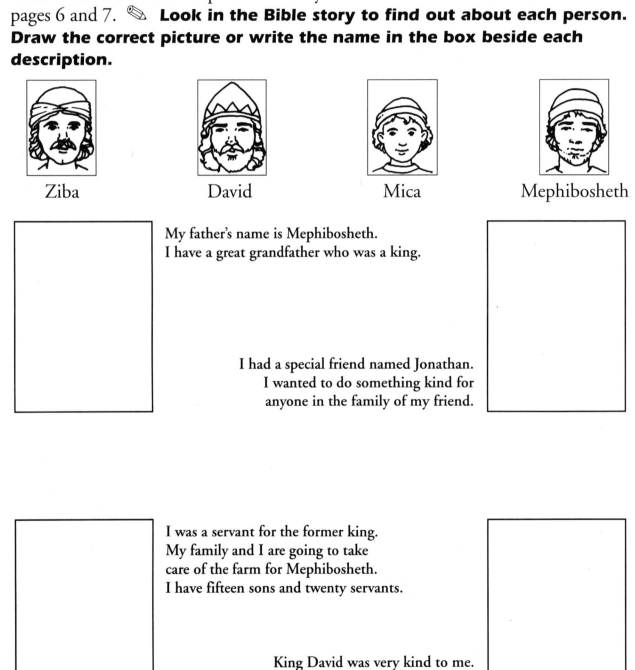

Ziba   David   Mica   Mephibosheth

My father's name is Mephibosheth.
I have a great grandfather who was a king.

I had a special friend named Jonathan.
I wanted to do something kind for
anyone in the family of my friend.

I was a servant for the former king.
My family and I are going to take
care of the farm for Mephibosheth.
I have fifteen sons and twenty servants.

King David was very kind to me.
King David gave me my grandfather's land.
My father's name was Jonathan.

PUPPETS FOR A PLAY ABOUT BEING KIND

Make puppets to use with the puppet play on pages 11 and 12.

You need:
- ☐ 4" x 6" cards
- ☐ Scissors
- ☐ Paper clips
- ☐ Markers
- ☐ Glue

✄ **To make Puppets:**

1. Cut (3) 4" x 6" cards in half to make (6) 2" x 6" strips.
2. Fold cards as indicated and secure with glue or paper clips.
3. Decorate and cut out puppets.
4. Glue one puppet to each index card.

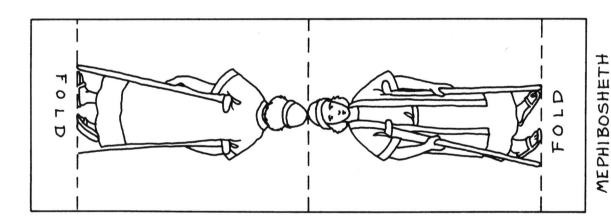

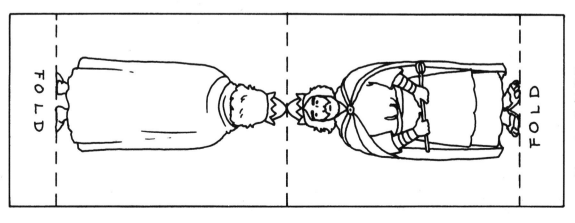

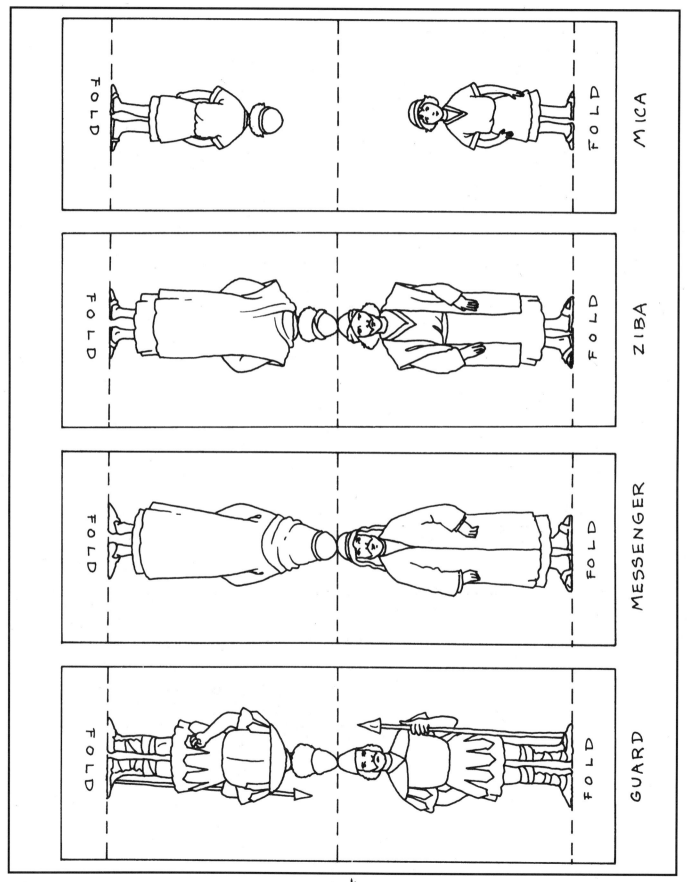

BEING KIND TO A FAMILY IN HIDING

A Puppet Play Based on 2 Samuel 9:1-13

In this true story are: King David, Mephibosheth (grandson of the former king, Saul), Mica, (Mephibosheth's son), Ziba (servant of the former king, Saul), a servant, and a guard.

PREPARATION: 1. Follow the directions for making the puppets on pages 9 and 10.
2. Use the patterns to make other puppets to be the people that were also a part of this story. (Ziba had fifteen sons and twenty servants. King David had many guards and servants living and working in the palace.)
3. Make your own background scenery.

SETTING: This takes place in the city of Jerusalem and in Lo Debar, a town probably about thirty miles east of Jerusalem.

[MICA and MEPHIBOSHETH are stage left, very close together.]

MICA *(whispering)*: Why do we have to stay here all the time? Can't we go somewhere else just for a few days? You can ride on the donkey so your legs don't get too tired.

MEPHIBOSHETH *(whispering)*: I'm sorry, Mica. But we can't go away from here. We need to be sure King David doesn't find us. We are safe here.

MICA: But all the people say King David is a good king. Why are we hiding from him?

MEPHIBOSHETH: We don't know what the king will do. He might want to kill me because of Saul. Saul was my grandfather. He was David's enemy, and David might think that I am his enemy, too.

MICA: Are you David's enemy?

MEPHIBOSHETH: No, Mica. We just want to be safe. We don't want anything to hurt King David. *(There is a loud knock.)* Shhhh! *(calling)* Who is it?

ZIBA: It is I, Ziba.

[MICA runs to the right side of the stage. ZIBA enters.]

MEPHIBOSHETH: Ziba! What are you doing here? Is something wrong?

ZIBA: I hope not! King David wants you to come to his palace.

MEPHIBOSHETH: What? How does he even know where I am? What does he want with me? It sounds like something is wrong!

ZIBA: No, I really don't think so. Listen, this is what happened. A messenger came to get me and took me to the king. King David asked me if there was anyone still living who was related to King Saul. So I told him about you.

MEPHIBOSHETH: But . . . I thought I would be safe . . . now I . . .

ZIBA:	I haven't told you all the news yet. The king wants you to come so he can be kind to you!
MEPHIBOSHETH:	Kind to me? The grandson of King Saul and the son of Jonathan? Did you tell him about my legs, that I was crippled when I fell when I was five years old? Does he know I have a hard time walking?
ZIBA:	Yes! The king and your father were good friends, remember. The king is doing this to honor your father, Jonathan.
MICA *(moving in close to MEPHIBOSHETH, jumping up and down, and pulling on his father's arm)*:	If the king wants to see you, you have to go, don't you? Can I come too? *(turns to ZIBA)* Don't you think I should go, Ziba?
MEPHIBOSHETH:	Yes, Mica and Ziba, if the king asks for me, I must go. We'll leave as soon as we can get ready.

[All exit left. KING DAVID enters stage right and is seated as if in the throne room. GUARD enters with MEPHIBOSHETH and they move slowly to come before the KING. MEPHIBOSHETH bows down in front of DAVID.]

DAVID:	Mephibosheth!
MEPHIBOSHETH:	I am your servant, O king, I will do whatever you ask.
DAVID:	Please don't be afraid. I wish you well, not harm. I want to show you kindness because of my friend and your father, Jonathan. I want to give back to you all the land that belonged to Saul.
MEPHIBOSHETH:	But who am I, that you should do this?
DAVID:	I also want you to live here and eat at my table and be a part of my family every day. *(calling to the SERVANT)* Please ask Ziba to come in. *(SERVANT leaves and returns with ZIBA)*
DAVID *(to ZIBA)*:	I have given your master's grandson everything that belonged to Saul and his family. You and your sons and your servants are to farm the land for him and bring in the crops, so that he will be well provided for. Oh, yes, and I have asked Mephibosheth to stay here and eat with us at our table.
ZIBA:	I, and my fifteen sons and twenty servants, will do whatever you, our king, command us to do. *(ZIBA and MEPHIBOSHETH bow and then exit.)*

[MEPHIBOSHETH enters right, moving slowly across the stage toward the left, as MICA enters left and runs up to him.]

MICA:	Was the king kind, Father? Do we have to go back and hide?
MEPHIBOSHETH:	No, Mica, we are going to live here instead. And, yes! King David is a very kind king!

[MICA and MEPHIBOSHETH exit.]

BE KIND INSTEAD OF PAYING BACK WHEN HURT

✎ **Match the words in the WORD BOX to each statement. Then write the letters in the numbered blanks at the bottom of the page to complete the Bible verse.**

WORD BOX: dive   glue   hot   knob
                rose   water   year

1. a flower with many petals __ __ __ __
                              3   6   1   4

2. wet and good to drink __ __ __ __ __
                          10 12 16 4   3

3. sticks things together __ __ __ __
                           11 13 2   4

4. use to open a door __ __ __ __
                       14 5   6   7

5. to go jump into water __ __ __ __
                          8   15 18 4

6. twelve months __ __ __ __
                  9   4   12 3

7. not cold __ __ __
             17 6   16

1 Thessalonians 5:15

Make __ __ __ __ that __ __ __ __ __ __ pays back
     1 2 3 4   5 6 7 6 8 9

__ __ __ __ __ for __ __ __ __ __ , but
10 3 6 5 11   10 3 6 5 11

__ __ __ __ __ __ try to be __ __ __ __ to each
12 13 10 12 9 1   14 15 5 8

__ __ __ __ __ and to __ __ __ __ __ __ __ __ else.
6 16 17 4 3   4 18 4 3 9 6 5 4

Tell about a time that you paid someone back with kindness even though they were unkind to you.

BEING KIND
WHEN YOU PLAY

LET'S STAY HERE AND PLAY!

I WANT TO GO FOR A RIDE IN THAT KID'S POCKET!

Circle the kind things you see in Parada Park. Put an X on what is not kind.

PARADA PARK

KEEP ADDING TO
YOUR BEING KIND CHAIN

Look for new and unusual ways to be kind. Every time you think of one or try one, write it on a link for this chain. See if you can make your chain go all the way around your room.

You need:
- ☐ (20-50) 3" x 5" colored index cards
- ☐ Ruler
- ☐ Pencil
- ☐ Scissors

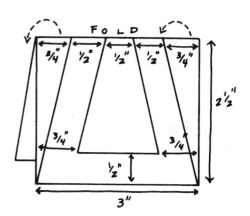

✂ To make a Being Kind Chain:

1. Use your ruler to make a pattern as shown in the illustrations.

2. Fold each 3" x 5" card, trace the pattern with the folded edge as marked, and cut out each chain link.

3. Join the links together by slipping one side of one link through the fold in another link. Slide the link on and down to the bottom on the link, as shown.

4. Continue adding as many links as you can.

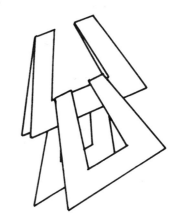

How do you find new ways to be kind?

1. Think about being kind.

2. Watch what other people do. (When you see someone doing a kind thing, make a note of it.)

3. Ask God to help you be kind.

 CAN WE MAKE A CHAIN LIKE THIS TO SWING FROM THAT TREE?

 LET'S TRY. I'LL READ THE DIRECTIONS.

HOW MANY WAYS TO BE KIND?

Are you looking for new ways to be kind? Add these ideas to your chain. (See page 15.)

- Smile at someone new at school.
- Be quiet when others are working.
- Don't wait to be asked to do the dishes.
- Feed a friend's pet when needed.
- Help others with schoolwork you are good at.

- Be polite and say "please."
- Offer to help a sad friend.
- Let another person go first.
- Help carry heavy packages.

✎ **Use these words to help you look for more kind things to add to your chain. To put them into the puzzle, start with the 6- and 7-letter words first.**

2 letters	4 letters		5 letters		6 letters	7 letters
do	give	nice	carry	share	remind	respect
	good	play	cheer	smile		
	help	talk	clean	start		
	lend	work	offer	thank		
	make					

"FROG" IS A KIND WORD.

I'LL GO JUMP IN THE LIST.

BE KIND TO ENEMIES

✏️ **Unscramble the words to the Bible verse, Luke 6:35. They are scrambled in groups of letters. The first letter for each missing word is in the MIDDLE of each scrambled letter group.**

But __ __ __ E your __ __ __ M __ __ __ , do

__ __ __ D to __ H __ __ , and L __ __ __ to

__ H __ __ without expecting to get

A __ __ __ __ __ __ __   __ __ C __ .

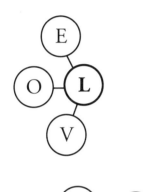

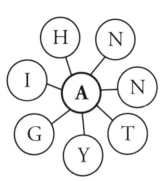

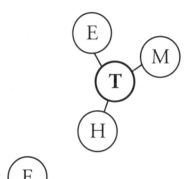

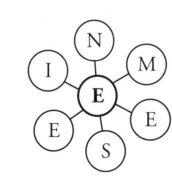

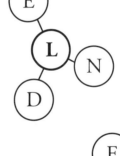

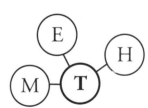

What is one way you can be kind to an "enemy"?

_____

Remember: While God wants us to be kind, that doesn't mean that you are to let someone hurt you.

GOD IS KIND EVEN TO PEOPLE WHO ARE MEAN.

I WISH MORE PEOPLE WERE LIKE HIM.

Kind to People in a Shipwreck

Acts 27:15, 27-44; 28:1-12

The ship was caught by the storm and could not head into the wind; so we gave way to it and were driven along. . . . On the fourteenth night we were still being driven across the Adriatic Sea, when about midnight the sailors sensed they were approaching land. . . .

Altogether there were 276 of us on board. . . . But the ship struck a sandbar and ran aground. The bow stuck fast and would not move, and the stern was broken to pieces by the pounding of the surf. . . .

[The Centurion] ordered those who could swim to jump overboard first and get to land. The rest were to get there on planks or on pieces of the ship. In this way everyone reached land in safety.

"ISLANDERS" ARE THE PEOPLE WHO LIVE ON AN ISLAND.

Once safely on shore, we found out that the island was called Malta. The islanders showed us unusual kindness. They built a fire and welcomed us all because it was raining and cold. . . .

(Read the rest of the story on page 19)

(Read the rest of the story on page 19)

✎ **Write YES or NO.**

_____ The ship was broken to pieces by the storm.

_____ Some of the people stayed on the ship and died.

_____ There were only fifteen people on the ship.

_____ Everyone on the ship reached land safely.

_____ The islanders were kind and built a fire.

_____ The name of the island was Malta.

_____ The islanders were unkind to the people in the shipwreck.

THE BIBLE TELLS ABOUT BEING KIND

Kind to People in a Shipwreck

(Acts 27:15,27-44; Acts 28:1-12 continued from page 18)

There was an estate nearby that belonged to Publius, the chief official of the island. He welcomed us to his home and for three days entertained us hospitably. His father was sick in bed, suffering from fever and dysentery. Paul went in to see him and, after prayer, placed his hands on him and healed him. When this had

AN "ESTATE" IS A BIG HOUSE WITH LOTS OF LAND AROUND IT.

happened, the rest of the sick on the island came and were cured. They honored us in many ways and when we were ready to sail, they furnished us with the supplies we needed.

"FURNISHED" MEANS THE PEOPLE GAVE THEM FOOD AND OTHER THINGS.

After three months we put out to sea in a ship that had wintered in the island.

✏️ **Tell what happened first in the story by writing 1, 2, 3 and so on in the boxes.**

The people on the ship safely made it to land.

Publius shared his home.

The food and other things they needed for the ship were given to them when they left.

Paul prayed for Publius's father, and God healed him.

For three months, the islanders took care of the people in the shipwreck.

The people on the island built a fire and welcomed those from the shipwreck.

THE BIBLE TELLS ABOUT BEING KIND

Kind to People in a Shipwreck

Read about the kind people on the island in your Bible in Acts 27:15, 27-44, and Acts 28:1-12, or on pages 18 and 19.

✎ **Write the number from the picture to show where each thing happened.**

_____ The ship was damaged by the storm.

_____ Publius shared his home.

_____ The people on the ship swam or floated safely to shore.

_____ The island people built a fire to make everyone warm.

✎ **Draw the people in the picture. Show the islanders being kind to Paul and the others.**

GIVE A BOWL OF KINDNESS

Make a container or bowl you can give away. Fill it with small apples, cookies, or colorful leaves.

You need:

☐ A round balloon, blown up and tied, about 10"-12" diameter (If a balloon doesn't work well, use a small cardboard box as your base object.)
☐ Wallpaper paste
☐ Large mixing bowl and spoon
☐ Newspaper
☐ Paper towels
☐ Poster paints and brushes
☐ Scissors

WE COULD MAKE ONE OF THESE FOR GRANDMA GREEN.

WE COULD MAKE IT UPSIDE DOWN. SO SHE COULD USE IT AS A NEW HOUSE.

✂ To make a Bowl of Kindness:

Note: The balloon will be the base object to form the shape of your bowl. For best results, add two layers of newspaper strips and then one layer of paper towel strips. Let each layer dry overnight before adding another layer of paper.

1. Mix the wallpaper paste with a small amount of warm water to form a thin consistency.
2. Tear several sheets of newspaper into 3" strips and several sheets of paper towel into 2" strips.
3. Soak some of the newspaper strips in the paste mixture. When they are completely wet, remove one strip at a time, rub off any extra paste and lay it over the balloon. Add strips, crisscrossing each other until the surface of more than half the balloon is covered. (The strips when dry will be your bowl.)
4. Allow this layer to dry and then add another layer of strips.
5. Use paper towels for the last layer of strips. When this layer is dry, remove the balloon, and cut the "bowl" around the top edge to make it even.
6. Paint the bowl inside and out. Let dry.

CHOOSING TO BE KIND

✎ **Here are some times in which you could choose to be kind. Draw or write what you would do in each.**

1. You are next in line at the drinking fountain. Someone comes up who's been running around the track. They are obviously hot and thirsty.

   What could you do?

   _____

   _____

2. Your sister is finishing the sewing on her costume for the school play, and it is her night to do the dishes. You finished your homework early and have a little free time.

   What could you do?

   _____

   _____

3. You arrive at Sunday school early and see your teacher setting up the chairs in a new way for class.

   What could you do?

   _____

   _____

THE VALUE OF BEING KIND

God's values are the STANDARD to help me know how to live my life and treat other people

HOW CAN YOU KNOW WHAT YOUR VALUES ARE? Look at the things you DO, SAY, and THINK. If you spend time doing something, then you know it is one of your values.

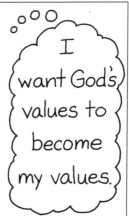

I want God's values to become my values.

✎ **Draw a picture of yourself here.** Are you thinking what is in the thought balloon?

My name is _____

Being kind _____ important to me.
            is   is not

I _____ spend time doing something nice for someone.
   do   do not

Doing something nice or helpful for another person is being kind.

I can show that being kind is becoming my value when

I _____ and _____

✎ **Make a treat and take it to your Sunday school or classroom teacher.**

BEING PURPOSEFUL IS . . . knowing what you want to do and being determined to do it.

I think purposeful can also mean _____

_____

✎ **Decorate this word with 3 different colors. Then, put the letter "P" on the line if the sentence is something a purposeful person might say.**

Purposeful

_____ "I've been practicing every day."

_____ "I won't even try."

_____ "It's too hard."

_____ "I know someone who can show me how to do it."

_____ "I will do it."

Being purposeful is important to me.
When I know what I want to do and I am determined to do it, then being purposeful becomes one of my values.

Name _____

Date _____

God's values are the STANDARD to help me know how to live my life and treat other people

THE BIBLE TELLS ABOUT BEING PURPOSEFUL

Jesus Decides to Do What His Father Asks

Matthew 26:36-44

Then Jesus went with his disciples to a place called Gethsemane, and he said to them, "Sit here while I go over there and pray." He took Peter and the two sons of Zebedee along with him, and he began to be sorrowful and troubled. Then he said to them, "My soul is overwhelmed with sorrow to the point of death. Stay here and keep watch with me."

"SORROWFUL" MEANS VERY SAD, FULL OF SORROW.

"THIS CUP" WAS ABOUT JESUS' DYING ON THE CROSS.

Going a little farther, he fell with his face to the ground and prayed, "My Father, if it is possible, may this cup be taken from me. Yet not as I will, but as you will."

(Read the rest of this story on page 26)

✎ **Write the correct word on each line.**

asleep Father Gethsemane

prayed sorrow three waited

1. Jesus and his disciples went to
_____.

2. The disciples sat down and _____ while Jesus took Peter and two others with him.

3. Jesus was filled with _____ .

4. Jesus put his face to the ground and _____.

5. Jesus prayed that He would do what His _____ wanted Him to do.

6. When Jesus came back, the disciples were _____.

7. Jesus went away to pray _____ times.

THE BIBLE TELLS ABOUT BEING PURPOSEFUL

Jesus Decides to Do What His Father Asks

(Matthew 26:36-44 continued from page 25)

Then he returned to his disciples and found them sleeping. "Could you men not keep watch with me for one hour?" he asked Peter. "Watch and pray so that you will not fall into temptation. The spirit is willing, but the body is weak."

He went away a second time and prayed, "My Father, if it is not possible for this cup to be taken away unless I drink it, may your will be done."

When he came back, he again found them sleeping, because their eyes were heavy. So he left them and went away once more and prayed the third time, saying the same thing.

"EYES WERE HEAVY" MEANS THE DISCIPLES WERE SO SLEEPY THEY COULDN'T KEEP THEIR EYES OPEN.

✎ **Use the letter box to fill in the missing words by going up and down the columns like this:**

Jesus made a ___ ___ ___ ___   ___ ___ ___ ___   ___ ___ ___ ___

___ ___ ___ ___ ___ ___ ___ ___ .

He said ___ ___   ___ ___ ___ ___ ___ ___ ___   ___ ___

___ ___ ___ ___   ___ ___ ___   ___ ___ ___ ___ ___ ___ ,

___ ___ ___ ___   ___ ___ ___ ___   ___ ___ ___   ___ ___ .

START	H	I	S	W	H	D	H
	A	C	I	O	A	N	E
	R	E	O	D	T	A	D
	D	D	N	D	G	D	I
	A	D	H	L	O	E	D
	N	A	E	U	D	K	I
	D	S	W	O	A	S	T	FINISH

THE BIBLE TELLS ABOUT BEING PURPOSEFUL

Jesus Decides to Do What His Father Asks

Jesus knew that God, His Father, asked Him to die on the cross. This was a very hard thing to do, but Jesus decided He would do whatever His Father asked Him to do. Read about Jesus in Gethsemane in your Bible in Matthew 26:36-44 or on pages 25 and 26.

✎ **Find these words about how Jesus was feeling in the Bible story. Circle the right meaning for each word or phrase.**

Jesus was

| sorrowful | singing and happy |
| | filled with sadness |

| troubled | very concerned and upset |
| | a problem |

| overwhelmed | not understanding |
| | completely overcome with concern |

When Jesus said, "may this cup be taken away unless I drink it," He was talking about

His death on the cross.

getting something to drink.

When Jesus said, "not as I will, but as you will," this meant

He would keep praying.

He would do what His Father wanted, instead of what He might have wished.

DO WHAT THE BIBLE SAYS

✎ **Use the CODE BOX to find the letters to the words of this Bible verse in James 1:22. Some letters have the same code, so think carefully before you write those letters. Note: each letter has two parts to the code. Read across and down to find the letter. For example [👦] 3 = T, [👧] 2 is either M or N.**

	1	2	3	4
👦	A	C/D	E	H/L
👧	I	M/N	O	R
👦	U/V	S	T	W/Y

    '

"MERELY" MEANS ONLY, JUST DO THIS PART.

   . James 1:22

"DECEIVE" IS TO MAKE SOMEONE THINK SOMETHING IS RIGHT WHEN IT ISN'T.

One thing you can DO that the Bible says is _____

WHAT TO DO NEXT

✎ **Can you help these two kids be purposeful in what they're doing? Write what you think these kids could do. Some ideas are given to help you get started.**

I wish I could learn how to ride a bike! I had a lesson last week, but I don't think I'll ever get it. What can I do now?

- Ask for another lesson.
- Practice every day.
- Forget learning to ride.

Write what you think Sharla could do:

_____

_____

_____

Do you know how to use a computer? We have one at school but I never get to use it. I know I'll need to know about it before I go to college. Do you have any ideas about how I can find a computer to use?

- Ask your teacher if you can use one at school in extra time.
- Start a family computer fund.
- Forget it.

Write what you think Doug could do:

_____

_____

_____

Be purposeful and plan a pizza party. Have everyone work together to make the refreshments for the party.

LOOK OUT! IF YOU HOP ON THAT CHEESE, YOU'RE TOASTED!

BUT I JUST WANT A BITE.

You need:

- ☐ Toaster oven or traditional oven
- ☐ Large (2-1/2" or larger) cookie cutters in shapes such as heart, star, cross, or circle
- ☐ Baking sheet
- ☐ Timer
- ☐ Bread sliced about 1/2" thick
- ☐ Cheese slice, mozzarella or other of your choice
- ☐ 1/8 cup pizza sauce
- ☐ Cutting board, knife, and oven mitt
- ☐ **OPTIONAL:** Toppings such as olive slices, mushroom pieces, pepperoni slices, and so on

✂ To make a Design Pizza:

1. Preheat broiler.

2. Choose a cookie cutter shape and use it to cut that shape out of a slice of bread and a slice of cheese.

3. Put the bread shape on a cookie sheet and broil it without any topping or cheese for 1-2 minutes on each side, just enough to slightly toast the bread.

4. Use the knife to spread a thin layer of pizza sauce on one side of the toasted shape, and put the cheese shape on top of the sauce.

5. Decorate the cheese with one or more of the toppings.

6. Put in broiler for about 2-3 minutes, until cheese begins to melt.

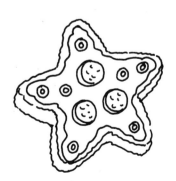

POP-UP NAME CARDS
FOR YOUR PIZZA PARTY

Honor the people at your Design Pizza Party with a pop-up card.

You need:

- ☐ 5" x 7" heavy white paper or construction paper (one for each person)
- ☐ Markers and scissors
- ☐ List of names of the people for the party

✂ To make Pop-up Name Cards:

1. Fold the paper in half (2-1/2" x 7").

2. Unfold the paper and write a name in large cursive letters above the fold, using the fold as the bottom line.

3. Use a contrasting color and draw a line around the top of the letters that follows the general outline of the name.

4. Being careful to leave the fold line uncut at the ends of the fold, poke one end of the scissors through the paper at the beginning of the name shape, and then cut around the outline of the name, as shown.

5. Bend the card on the fold so the name pops up and the fold bends backward so the card can stand upright.

6. Use markers to decorate the card as you wish.

7. Continue until you have made a Pop-Up Name Card for everyone.

SERVE GOD NO MATTER WHAT!

✎ **In the word search, circle all the words underlined in this Bible verse that you can find. Some will be missing. When you discover which ones are missing, write them in the right order on the lines below.**

The Bible verse 1 Corinthians 15:58 says

<u>Stand</u> <u>firm</u>. <u>Let</u> <u>nothing</u> <u>move</u> you. <u>Always</u> <u>give</u> <u>yourselves</u> <u>fully</u> to <u>the</u> <u>work</u> <u>of</u> the

<u>Lord,</u> <u>because</u> you <u>know</u> <u>that</u> your <u>labor</u> in the Lord <u>is</u> not in <u>vain</u>.

"LABOR" IS THE WORK AND OTHER THINGS YOU DO.

```
A L W A Y S B Q E V O M
C J N K X C D L A B O R
L Y O U R S E L V E S B
E F T L K B X Q J C S D
T K H Q M N H T H A T N
V A I N J M O D F U V A
M W N K X F G W I S N T
G F G J F I R M C E Q S
F U L L Y V B D K P Z F
```

"NOT IN VAIN" MEANS IT WILL NOT BE WASTED.

<u>W</u> __ __ __   for   __ __ __   __ __ __ __ ,

and do not   <u>G</u> __ __ __   up.

What would you say when you explain to a friend what it means to "stand firm" for God?

_____

LEARNING SOMETHING NEW FOR FUN

Look for a new game to learn, a new sport to play, or a new skill to practice. Be purposeful until you can do your best at it.

Learn to be a JUGGLER

You need:
- ☐ 3 or more old socks
- ☐ Fabric paints or crayons
- ☐ Old newspapers

 To make Juggling Balls:
1. Decorate the socks with fabric crayons or paints. If you use paints, let dry before going on to the next step.
2. Fill each sock with crumpled newspapers and fold in the end.
3. Practice using two balls until you have a smooth rhythm.
4. Add a third ball to your circular motion and keep practicing.
5. Go to the library and find out more about your new skill of juggling.

Play OUTDOOR WATER BALLOON TAG

You need:
- ☐ 1 or more friends
- ☐ A balloon for each person
- ☐ 15" piece of string for each person
- ☐ Water source

 **To play:**
1. Fill each balloon about half full of water, add a little air to the balloon, and tie the end.
2. Attach one end of the string to the balloon and the other end around one ankle.
3. The object of the game is to pop the other player's balloon while keeping your own balloon from being broken.
4. Feet are the only objects that can be used to break the balloons.
5. Play until only one person has a balloon still filled with water.

✎ **What are some things you would like to do, need to do, or want to learn to do? Use the word PURPOSEFUL to help you write a list. Then be purposeful and get started!**

_____ **P** _____

_____ **U** _____

_____ Write a lette **R** every week to my grandparents _____

_____ **P** _____

_____ **O** _____

_____ **S** _____

_____ **E** _____

_____ **F** _____

_____ **U** _____

_____ **L** earn how to paint _____

CAN YOU
WRITE
FROG
LONG
JUMP
OVER THERE
BY THE F?

GOOD
IDEA, WE
NEED THE
PRACTICE.

KEEP ON UNTIL YOU FINISH

✎ **When you are purposeful you plan to do something, and then do it! Draw the missing picture in each of these situations.**

Joshua Chooses to Serve God

Joshua 24:1-26

Then Joshua assembled all the tribes of Israel at Shechem. He summoned the elders, leaders, judges and officials of Israel, and they presented themselves before God.

Joshua said to all the people, "This is what the LORD, the God of Israel, says: 'Long ago your forefathers, including Terah the father of Abraham and Nahor, lived beyond the River and worshiped other gods. But I took your father Abraham from the land beyond the River and led him throughout Canaan and gave him many descendants. . . .

"When I brought your fathers out of Egypt, you came to the sea . . . Then you lived in the desert for a long time. . . .

"Then you crossed the Jordan and came to Jericho. The citizens of Jericho fought against you . . . but I gave them into your hands. . . . You did not do it with your own sword and bow. So I gave you a land on which you did not toil and cities you did not build; and you live in them and eat from vineyards and olive groves that you did not plant.'

"UNDESIRABLE" MEANS IT IS NOT GOOD, NOT WORTH IT.

A "HOUSEHOLD" IS A FAMILY AND THE OTHER PEOPLE LIVING AND WORKING TOGETHER.

"Now fear the LORD and serve him with all faithfulness. Throw away the gods your forefathers worshiped beyond the River and in Egypt, and serve the LORD. But if serving the LORD seems undesirable to you, then choose for yourselves this day whom you will serve . . . But as for me and my household, we will serve the LORD."

(Read the rest of this story on page 37)

CODE:
B	C	E	H	I	L
O	R	S	V	W	Y

✎ **Fill in the blanks below by using this code.** Hint: The letter above the line is the code for the letter just below it AND the letter below the line is the code for the letter above it!

Remember how God has always taken care of us.

Now we must _____ if
R-V-B-B-E-S

we will _____ and
E-S-C-H-S

_____ God.
B-O-S-L

I know my choice! My family and I _____ _____ the Lord.
I-W-Y-Y   E-S-C-H-S

THE BIBLE TELLS ABOUT BEING PURPOSEFUL

Joshua Chooses to Serve God

(Joshua 24:1-26 continued from page 36)

Then the people answered, "Far be it from us to forsake the LORD to serve other gods! It was the LORD our God himself who . . . protected us on our entire journey. . . . We too will serve the LORD, because he is our God."

Joshua said to the people, " . . . If you forsake the LORD and serve foreign gods, he will turn and bring disaster on you and make an end of you, after he has been good to you."

"FORSAKE" IS TO GIVE SOMETHING UP COMPLETELY.

But the people said to Joshua, "No! We will serve the LORD."

Then Joshua said, "You are witnesses against yourselves that you have chosen to serve the LORD."

"Yes, we are witnesses," they replied.

"Now then," said Joshua, "throw away the foreign gods that are among you and yield your hearts to the LORD, the God of Israel."

And the people said to Joshua, "We will serve the LORD our God and obey him."

A "COVENANT" IS A PROMISE. On that day Joshua made a covenant for the people, and there at Shechem he drew up for them decrees and laws. And Joshua record-ed these things in the Book of the Law of God.

✏️ **The people told Joshua what they would do. Start at the word WE and draw a line connecting letters to find what the people said. Lines can go up, down, right, or left. Write the words on the lines and underline them in the story.**

K	E	V	R	E	S	L	F	Q	D	C	W
V	T	P	X	C	J	L	J	B	F	M	E
K	H	D	G	Q	C	I	Z	P	G	O	D
G	E	S	J	¹<u>W</u>	<u>E</u>	W	K	H	Y	X	Q
J	L	R	F	K	J	S	L	P	E	C	W
K	O	G	K	S	L	P	J	H	B	C	U
X	R	J	²<u>W</u>	<u>E</u>	W	I	L	L	O	M	J
W	D	M	X	C	K	F	G	L	J	Q	K

1. W E __ __ __ __ __   __ __ __ __   __ __ __   __ __ __ __ __ __ .

2. W E __ __ __ __   __ __ __ __   __ __ __ __ .

Joshua said: If the people choose to serve God, then they must keep doing it and not change their minds.

Joshua Chooses to Serve God

Read about Joshua being purposeful in your Bible in Joshua 24:1-26 or on pages 36 and 37.

Joshua told the people to remember how God had protected them, brought them safely to a new land, and taken care of them in everything they did.

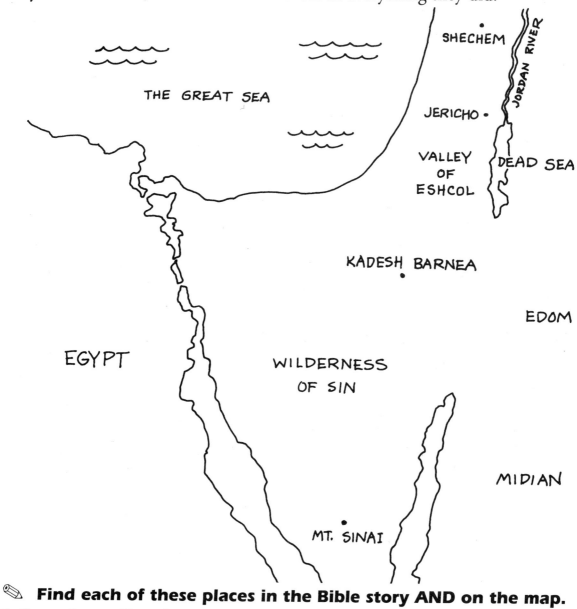

✎ **Find each of these places in the Bible story AND on the map.**
Follow these directions:

1. Put a * by EGYPT.

2. Draw a ▢ around JERICHO.

3. Draw an ⬭ around SHECHEM.

4. Put an X on the JORDAN RIVER.

DECIDING WHAT TO DO

✎ **Use this code to fill in the blanks. Draw a picture of yourself when you see a box. This will help remind you what being purposeful is.**

CODE:

⚀ = A   ⠆ = C   ⠌ = D   ⠿ = E   ⠪ = G   ⠿ = H   ✛ = I

⠿ = K   ⠿ = O   ‖ = R   ⠿ = W   ⠿ = T   ⠿ = M   ⠿ = N

You are purposeful when

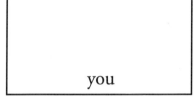
you

I'M STILL PRACTICING THE LONG JUMP.

what to ___ ___ , and then

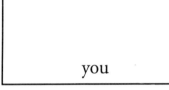
you

___ ___ ___ ___ ___ ___ ___ ___ ___ to ___ ___ it.

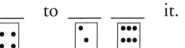

✎ **Put an X by something you might want to do.**

_____ 1. Learn to do a new sport, like _____

_____ 2. Write the best report I've ever written.

_____ 3. Earn money to go to camp.

_____ 4. Other _____

CAN YOU JUMP OVER THE POND YET?

God wants you to be purposeful about the things you do with your life. Can you do something to serve God? Here are some ideas.

1. S
   H
   O
   W other people what God is like by your **ACTIONS** and your W
                                                                   O
                                                                   R
                                                                   D
                                              R   S
                                              E
                                              A
2. Get to **KNOW** God better. D your Bible, pray every day, and
   go to **CHURCH**.

3. **ASK** God what He **WANTS** you to do with your life.

4. T
   A
   L
   K to other people about God and His S
                                        O
                                        N, Jesus.

5. Be God's **FRIEND**.

✎ **Put the WORDS IN ALL CAPITAL LETTERS in the crossword puzzle. The way the letters are written can help you know where each word should go.**

One way you can be God's friend is to

_____

_____

CAN YOU
STAND UP
LIKE THIS F
           R
           O
           G

NO, I'M A
FROG,
REMEMBER?

THE BEST WAY TO BE PURPOSEFUL

✎ **The Bible gives some good words about being purposeful. Fill in the words from the word box. Match the letter with a number to the number on the lines at the bottom of the page.**

> WORD BOX:
>
> | do | fought | strength |
> | everything | hand | whatever |
> | faith | gives | your |
> | finished | might | |

1. I can do ___ ___ ___ ___ ___ ___ ___ ___ ___ _G_ through

           8

   him [Christ] who ___ ___ ___ ___ _S_ me

           9

   ___ ___ ___ ___ ___ ___ ___ ___ _H_ . Philippians 4:13

   4

THE BIBLE HELPS KIDS WHEN THEY WANT TO BE PURPOSEFUL.

2. ___ ___ ___ ___ ___ ___ ___ ___ _R_ your ___ ___ ___ _D_ finds to do,

     1   2

   ___ _O_ it with all ___ ___ ___ _R_ ___ ___ ___ ___ _T_ . Ecclesiastes 9:10

   10   3   5

3. [Paul said], "I have ___ ___ ___ ___ ___ _T_ the good

           6

   fight, I have ___ ___ ___ ___ ___ ___ ___ ___ _D_ the race,

          7

   I have kept the ___ ___ ___ ___ _H_ ." 2 Timothy 4:7

- -

Be purposeful in ___ ___ ___ ___ that ___ ___ ___ ___ ___   ___ ___ ___ !

                      1 2 3 4   5 6 7 6 8   9 6 10

What is one thing you can do to honor God? _____

THE VALUE OF BEING PURPOSEFUL

God's values are the STANDARD to help me know how to live my life and treat other people

HOW CAN YOU KNOW WHAT YOUR VALUES ARE?
Look at the things you DO, SAY, and THINK. If you spend time doing something, then you know it is one of your values.

I want God's values to become my values.

Are you thinking what is in the thought balloon?

My name is _____

Being purposeful _____ important to me.
<u>is   is not</u>

I _____ spend time deciding what I want to do and then doing it.
<u>do   do not</u>

Knowing what I want to do and being determined to do it is being purposeful.

I can show that being purposeful is becoming my value when I _____

_____ and _____

✎ **Write a letter to an adult who is working at a job you want to know more about.**
This is one way you can be purposeful about finding out what God may have for you in your future.

VALUE BUILDERS SERIES INDEX
BY VALUE

Accepting
Romans 15:7
Galatians 3:28
Luke 7 — Jesus and the woman with no name
Acts 10 — Peter's vision and visit

Appreciative
See thankful

Attentive
Psalm 34:15
James 1:19
Nehemiah 8 — Ezra reads the law
Luke 10 — Mary listens to Jesus

Caring
See concerned

Choices
See wise

Committed
1 Kings 8:61
Proverbs 16:3
Esther 4 — Esther
John 1 — Andrew follows Jesus

Compassionate
2 Corinthians 1:3-4
1 Peter 3:8
Luke 10 — Good Samaritan
Luke 23 — Jesus on the cross

Concerned
1 Corinthians 12:25
1 John 3:17
Matthew 25 — Jesus teaches to meet needs
Acts 2 — Church provides for each other

Confident
Philippians 4:13
Psalm 139:14
1 Samuel 17 — David and Goliath
Nehemiah 6 — Nehemiah isn't intimidated

Considerate
See respectful, kind

Consistent
1 John 3:18
Psalm 33:4
Matthew 26 — Jesus in the garden
Daniel 6 — Daniel as administrator

Contented
See peaceful

Conviction
Deuteronomy 13:6-8
Acts 4:19-20
Daniel 3 — Blazing furnace and three Hebrews
John 2 — Jesus clears the temple courts

Cooperative
Colossians 3:23-24
Ephesians 4:16
Acts 6 — Disciples share responsibilities
Exodus 18 — Jethro gives Moses a plan

Courageous
Joshua 1:9
Isaiah 41:10
Acts 23 — Paul's nephew
Esther 4 — Esther

Creative
See resourceful

Decision Making
See purposeful

Dedicated
See committed

Dependable
See responsible

Diligent
See persevering, purposeful, responsible

Discerning
See wise

Discipleship
See teachable, prayerful, worshipful, faith, holy

Discipline
See self-disciplined

Empathy
Galatians 6:2
Hebrews 13:3
John 11 — Jesus at Lazarus's death
1 Samuel 19 — Jonathan speaks up for David

Endurance
See persevering, self-disciplined, purposeful

Enthusiasm
See joyful

Fairness
Leviticus 19:15
Romans 12:17
James 2 — Favoritism at a meeting
Matthew 20 — Parable of workers

Faith
John 3:16
Hebrews 11:6
Acts 16 — Philippian jailer
Matthew 8 — Centurion sends servant to Jesus

Faithful
See loyal

VALUE BUILDERS SERIES INDEX
BY VALUE

Fellowship
See friendly

Flexibility
See cooperative, initiative, resourceful

Forgiving
Ephesians 4:32
Leviticus 19:18
Matthew 18   Parable of unforgiving servant
Genesis 45   Joseph forgives brothers

Friendly
Luke 6:31
Proverbs 17:17
1 Samuel 18   David and Jonathan
Acts 9   Paul and Barnabas

Generosity
Matthew 5:42
Hebrews 13:16
Ruth 2   Boaz gives grain to Ruth
2 Corinthians 8   Paul's letter about sharing

Gentle
Matthew 11:29-30
Philippians 4:5
Mark 10   Jesus and the children
John 19   Joseph of Arimathea prepares Jesus' body

Genuineness
See sincerity

Giving
See generosity

Goodness
See consistent, holy

Helpfulness
Acts 20:35
Ephesians 6:7-8
Exodus 2   Miriam and baby Moses
Mark 14   Disciples prepare Last Supper

Holy
1 Peter 1:15
Psalm 51:10
Acts 10   Cornelius
Exodus 3   Moses and the burning bush

Honest
Leviticus 19:11
Ephesians 4:25
Mark 14   Peter lies about knowing Jesus
1 Samuel 3   Samuel tells Eli the truth

Honor
See obedient, respectful, reverence

Hopeful
Jeremiah 29:11
Romans 15:13
Acts 1   Jesus will return/Ascension
Genesis 15   Abraham looks to the future

Humble
Psalm 25:9
Romans 12:16
Luke 7   Centurion asks Jesus to heal son
Matthew 3   John the Baptist and Jesus

Independent
See confident, initiative

Initiative
Joshua 22:5
Ephesians 4:29
John 13   Jesus washes feet
Nehemiah 2   Nehemiah asks to go to Jerusalem

Integrity
See consistent, holy, honest

Joyful
1 Thessalonians 5:16
1 Peter 1:8
Luke 2   Jesus' birth
Acts 12   Rhoda greets Peter

Justice
See fairness

Kind
1 Thessalonians 5:15
Luke 6:35
2 Samuel 9   David and Mephibosheth
Acts 28   Malta islanders and Paul

Knowledge
See teachable

Listening
See attentive

Long-suffering
See patience

Loving
John 13:34-35
1 Corinthians 13:4-7
Luke 15   Prodigal son
John 11   Mary, Martha, Lazarus and Jesus

Loyal
1 Chronicles 29:18
Romans 12:5
1 Samuel 20   David and Jonathan
Ruth 1   Ruth and Naomi

Meek
See gentle, humble

VALUE BUILDERS SERIES INDEX
BY VALUE

Merciful
Psalm 103:10
Micah 6:8
1 Samuel 25 — Abigail helps David show mercy
Matthew 18 — Unmerciful servant

Obedient
See also respectful
1 Samuel 15:22
Ephesians 6:1
1 Samuel 17 — David takes lunch
Acts 9 — Ananias at Saul's conversion

Patience
Psalm 37: 7
Ephesians 4:2
Genesis 26 — Isaac opens new wells
Nehemiah 6 — Nehemiah stands firm

Peaceful
John 14:27
Hebrews 13:5-6
Acts 12 — Peter sleeping in prison
Matthew 6 — Jesus teaches contentment

Peer pressure, response to
See confident, conviction, wise

Persevering
Galatians 6:9
James 1:2-3
Acts 27 — Paul in shipwreck
Exodus 5 — Moses doesn't give up

Praise
See prayerful, thankful, worshipful

Prayerful
Philippians 4:6
James 5:16
Luke 11 — Jesus teaches disciples
Daniel 6 — Daniel prays daily

Pure
See holy

Purposeful
James 1:22
1 Corinthians 15:58
Matthew 26 — Jesus in Gethsemane
Joshua 24 — Joshua serves God

Reliable
See responsible

Repentant
Acts 26:20
1 John 1:9
Luke 15 — Prodigal son
Luke 22 — Peter's denial

Resourceful
Philippians 4:9
1 Peter 4:10
Luke 5 — Man lowered through roof
Luke 19 — Zacchaeus

Respectful
Deuteronomy 5:16
1 Peter 2:17
1 Samuel 26 — David doesn't kill Saul
Acts 16 — Lydia and other believers

Responsible
Galatians 6:4-5
Proverbs 20:11
Acts 20 — Paul continues his work
Numbers 13 — Caleb follows instructions

Reverence
Daniel 6:26-27
Psalm 78:4, 7
Daniel 3 — Blazing furnace and three Hebrews
Matthew 21 — Triumphal entry

Self-controlled
See self-disciplined

Self-disciplined
1 Timothy 4:7-8
2 Timothy 1:7
Daniel 1 — Daniel and king's meat
John 19 — Jesus was mocked

Self-esteem
See confident

Sensitivity
See empathy, compassionate, concerned, kind

Service (servanthood)
See cooperative, generosity, helpful, stewardship

Sharing
See generosity, stewardship

Sincerity
Romans 12:9
Job 33:3
Mark 5 — Jairus and his daughter
2 Timothy 1 — Timothy

Stewardship
Luke 3:11
Ephesians 5:15-16
2 Chronicles 31 — Temple contributions
Acts 4 — Believers share

Submission
See humble, respectful, self-disciplined

Supportive
See friendly, loving

Sympathy
See compassionate, concerned

Teachable
Joshua 1:8
Psalm 32:8
Luke 2   Young Jesus in the temple
Acts 18   Apollos with Priscilla and Aquila

Thankful
Psalm 28:17
Colossians 3:17
1 Chronicles 29   Celebrating the temple
Romans 16   Paul thanks Phoebe, Priscilla and
                         Aquila

Tolerant
See accepting

Trusting
Proverbs 3:5-6
Psalm 9:10
Acts 27   Sailors with Paul in shipwreck
2 Kings 18   Hezekiah trusts God

Trustworthiness
See honest, responsible

Truthful
See honest

Unselfish
Romans 15:1-3
Philippians 2:4
Luke 23   God gives His Son
John 6   Boy gives lunch

Wise
Proverbs 8:10
James 3:13
1 Kings 3   Solomon asks for wisdom
Daniel 1   Daniel and king's meat

Worshipful
Psalm 86:12
Psalm 122:1
Nehemiah 8   Ezra and the people worship
Acts 16   Paul and Silas in jail

Scripture	Story	Value
Genesis 15	Abraham looks to future	Hopeful
Genesis 26	Isaac opens new wells	Patience
Genesis 45	Joseph forgives brothers	Forgiving
Exodus 2	Miriam and baby Moses	Helpful
Exodus 3	Moses and the burning bush	Holy
Exodus 5	Moses doesn't give up	Persevering
Exodus 18	Jethro gives Moses a plan	Cooperative
Leviticus 19:11		Honest
Leviticus 19:15		Fairness
Leviticus 19:18		Forgiving
Numbers 13	Caleb follows instructions	Responsible
Deuteronomy 5:16		Respectful
Deuteronomy 13:6-8		Conviction
Joshua 1:8		Teachable
Joshua 1:9		Courageous
Joshua 22:5		Initiative
Joshua 24	Joshua serves God	Purposeful
Ruth 1	Ruth and Naomi	Loyal
Ruth 2	Boaz gives grain to Ruth	Generosity
1 Samuel 3	Samuel tells Eli the truth	Honest
1 Samuel 15:22		Obedient
1 Samuel 17	David and Goliath	Confident
1 Samuel 17	David takes lunch	Obedient
1 Samuel 18	David and Jonathan	Friendly
1 Samuel 19	Jonathan speaks up for David	Empathy
1 Samuel 20	David and Jonathan	Loyal
1 Samuel 25	Abigail helps David show mercy	Merciful
1 Samuel 26	David doesn't kill Saul	Respectful
2 Samuel 9	David and Mephibosheth	Kind
1 Kings 3	Solomon asks for wisdom	Wise
1 Kings 8:61		Committed
2 Kings 18	Hezekiah trusts God	Trusting
1 Chronicles 29	Celebrating the temple	Thankful
1 Chronicles 29:18		Loyal
2 Chronicles 31	Temple contributions	Stewardship
Nehemiah 2	Nehemiah asks to go to Jerusalem	Initiative
Nehemiah 6	Nehemiah isn't intimidated	Confident
Nehemiah 6	Nehemiah stands firm	Patience
Nehemiah 8	Ezra and the people worship	Worshipful
Nehemiah 8	Ezra reads the law	Attentive
Esther 4	Esther	Committed
Esther 4	Esther	Courageous
Job 33:3		Sincerity

Scripture	Story	Value
Psalm 9:10		Trusting
Psalm 25:9		Humble
Psalm 28:17		Thankful
Psalm 32:8		Teachable
Psalm 33:4		Consistent
Psalm 34:15		Attentive
Psalm 37:7		Patience
Psalm 51:10		Holy
Psalm 78:4, 7		Reverence
Psalm 86:12		Worshipful
Psalm 103:10		Merciful
Psalm 122:1		Worshipful
Psalm 139:14		Confident
Proverbs 3:5-6		Trusting
Proverbs 8:10		Wise
Proverbs 16:3		Committed
Proverbs 17:17		Friendly
Proverbs 20:11		Responsible
Isaiah 41:10		Courageous
Jeremiah 29:11		Hopeful
Daniel 1	Daniel and king's meat	Self-disciplined
Daniel 1	Daniel and king's meat	Wise
Daniel 3	Blazing furnace and three Hebrews	Conviction
Daniel 3	Blazing furnace and three Hebrews	Reverence
Daniel 6	Daniel as administrator	Consistent
Daniel 6	Daniel prays daily	Prayerful
Daniel 6:26-27		Reverence
Micah 6:8		Merciful
Matthew 3	John the Baptist and Jesus	Humble
Matthew 5:42		Generosity
Matthew 6	Jesus teaches contentment	Peaceful
Matthew 8	Centurion sends servant to Jesus	Faith
Matthew 11:29-30		Gentle
Matthew 18	Unmerciful servant	Merciful
Matthew 18	Parable of unforgiving servant	Forgiving
Matthew 20	Parable of workers	Fairness
Matthew 21	Triumphal entry	Reverence
Matthew 25	Jesus teaches to meet needs	Concerned
Matthew 26	Jesus in Gethsemane	Purposeful
Matthew 26	Jesus in the garden	Consistent
Mark 5	Jairus and his daughter	Sincerity
Mark 10	Jesus and the children	Gentle
Mark 14	Disciples prepare Last Supper	Helpful
Mark 14	Peter lies about knowing Jesus	Honest
Luke 2	Jesus' birth	Joyful
Luke 2	Young Jesus in the temple	Teachable
Luke 3:11		Stewardship
Luke 5	Man lowered through roof	Resourceful
Luke 6:31		Friendly
Luke 6:35		Kind

Luke 7	Centurion asks Jesus to heal son	Humble		1 Corinthians 12:25		Concerned
Luke 7	Jesus and woman with no name	Accepting		1 Corinthians 13:4-7		Loving
Luke 10	Good Samaritan	Compassionate		1 Corinthians 15:58		Purposeful
Luke 10	Mary listens to Jesus	Attentive				
Luke 11	Jesus teaches disciples	Prayerful		2 Corinthians 1:3-4		Compassionate
Luke 15	Prodigal son	Loving		2 Corinthians 8	Paul's letter about sharing	Generosity
Luke 15	Prodigal son	Repentant				
Luke 19	Zacchaeus	Resourceful		Galatians 3:28		Accepting
Luke 22	Peter's denial	Repentant		Galatians 6:2		Empathy
Luke 23	God gives His Son	Unselfish		Galatians 6:4-5		Responsible
Luke 23	Jesus on the cross	Compassionate		Galatians 6:9		Persevering
John 1	Andrew follows Jesus	Committed		Ephesians 4:2		Patience
John 2	Jesus clears the temple courts	Conviction		Ephesians 4:16		Cooperative
John 3:16		Faith		Ephesians 4:25		Honest
John 6	Boy gives lunch	Unselfish		Ephesians 4:29		Initiative
John 11	Jesus at Lazarus's death	Empathy		Ephesians 4:32		Forgiving
John 11	Mary, Martha, Lazarus, and Jesus	Loving		Ephesians 5:15-16		Stewardship
John 13	Jesus washes feet	Initiative		Ephesians 6:1		Obedient
John 13:34-35		Loving		Ephesians 6:7-8		Helpful
John 14:27		Peaceful				
John 19	Jesus is mocked	Self-disciplined		Philippians 2:4		Unselfish
John 19	Joseph of Arimathea prepares Jesus' body	Gentle		Philippians 4:5		Gentle
				Philippians 4:6		Prayerful
				Philippians 4:9		Resourceful
Acts 1	Jesus will return/Ascension	Hopeful		Philippians 4:13		Confident
Acts 2	Church provides for each other	Concerned				
Acts 4	Believers share	Stewardship		Colossians 3:17		Thankful
Acts 4:19-20		Conviction		Colossians 3:23-24		Cooperative
Acts 6	Disciples share responsibilities	Cooperative				
Acts 9	Ananias at Saul's conversion	Obedient		1 Thessalonians 5:15		Kind
Acts 9	Paul and Barnabas	Friendly		1 Thessalonians 5:16		Joyful
Acts 10	Cornelius	Holy		1 Timothy 4:7-8		Self-disciplined
Acts 10	Peter's vision and visit	Accepting				
Acts 12	Peter sleeping in prison	Peaceful		2 Timothy 1	Timothy	Sincerity
Acts 12	Rhoda greets Peter	Joyful		2 Timothy 1:7		Self-disciplined
Acts 16	Paul and Silas in jail	Worshipful				
Acts 16	Philippian jailer	Faith		Hebrews 11:6		Faith
Acts 16	Lydia and other believers	Respectful		Hebrews 13:3		Empathy
Acts 18	Apollos with Priscilla and Aquila	Teachable		Hebrews 13:5-6		Peaceful
Acts 20	Paul continues his work	Responsible		Hebrews 13:16		Generosity
Acts 20:35		Helpful				
Acts 23	Paul's nephew	Courageous		James 1:2-3		Persevering
Acts 26:20		Repentant		James 1:19		Attentive
Acts 27	Paul in a shipwreck	Persevering		James 1:22		Purposeful
Acts 27	Sailors with Paul in shipwreck	Trusting		James 2	Favoritism at a meeting	Fairness
Acts 28	Malta islanders with Paul	Kind		James 3:13		Wise
				James 5:16		Prayerful
Romans 12:5		Loyal				
Romans 12:9		Sincerity		1 Peter 1:8		Joyful
Romans 12:16		Humble		1 Peter 1:15		Holy
Romans 12:17		Fairness		1 Peter 2:17		Respectful
Romans 15:1-3		Unselfish		1 Peter 3:8		Compassionate
Romans 15:7		Accepting		1 Peter 4:10		Resourceful
Romans 15:13		Hopeful				
Romans 16	Paul thanks Phoebe, Priscilla, and Aquila	Thankful		1 John 1:9		Repentant
				1 John 3:17		Concerned
				1 John 3:18		Consistent